MISSION XTREME 3D

FLYING
MACHINES

Right eye

Right eye

Left eye

Left eye

MISSION XTREME 3D

FLYING MACHINES

Strap yourself in and get ready for an extreme mission to spot some wonders of the aeronautical world!

DANGER

FLIGHT CADET

cadet name:

i.d. number:

squadron:

special skill:

signature:

MISSION BRIEFING

1. Fill in the Flight Cadet form above.

2. Follow mission route .....> to complete task stages.

3. Use Xtreme 3D glasses to experience the ultimate flying adventure.

4. Finish your Xtreme mission by answering the DEBRIEF questions.

A replica of the Curtiss Pusher

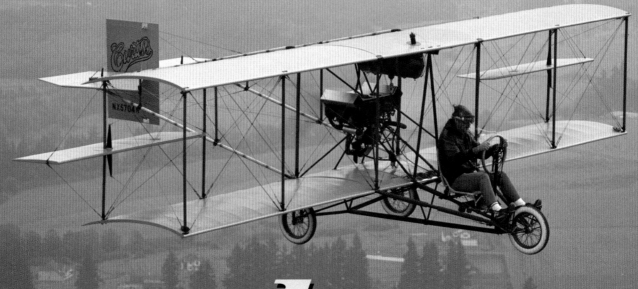

early FLYERS

> EARLY FLYING MACHINES were flimsy affairs that only the brave or reckless would risk flying. When World War One started those in command soon realized the military advantages aircraft could bring. It wasn't long before the first aerial battles were being witnessed. Dramatic dog fights made heroes of brave pilots who had little regard for their own safety – especially because parachutes had yet to be invented!

Focker Triplane

Curtiss Jenny

De Havilland Tigermoth

MISSION XTREME 3D

EARLY FLYERS

Q1. Who made the first powered flight?

Q2. How long did it last?

Q3. Who was first to fly across the English Channel?

Q4. What was the name of the first plane to be flown solo across the Atlantic?

DEBRIEF

Vought-Sikorsky prototype helicopter

FLYING MACHINES

The Wright brothers' airplane Flyer 1 makes its historic first flight

> TWELVE SECONDS is all it took for Orville Wright to change all our lives. Just south of Kittyhawk, North Carolina at 10.35am on Thursday, December 17, 1903, in Flyer 1, an aircraft designed and built by Orville and his brother Wilbur, he became the first man to make a powered flight. What follows is a procession of development, innovation, frustration and celebration as we take to the skies!

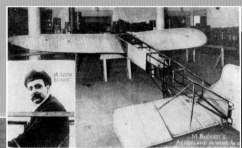

In 1909, Louis Blériot won the race to be the first person to fly across the English Channel...

...18 years later the first solo transatlantic flight was made in 1927 by Captain Charles Lindebergh in the "Spirit of St. Louis"

A replica Vickers Vimy takes to the air

Debrief answers: 1. Orville Wright. 2. 12 seconds. 3. Louis Blériot. 4. Spirit of St. Louis.

MISSION XTREME 3D

5

DANGER

Fighter
ACES

> FIGHTER PILOTS have the glamour image in air forces around the world. Jumping aboard their high-speed stallions they fly off to do battle in the skies above like high-altitude knights in shining armor. In the summer of 1940, during the Second World War's most famous air conflict – the Battle of Britain – a few hundred plucky Royal Air Force (RAF) pilots took on the might of the German Luftwaffe. The allies, with help from Polish, Canadian and New Zealand pilots, fought for Britain and the free world in their famous Spitfires and Hurricanes.

The Hawker Hurricane was the most successful allied fighter plane

Mitsubishi Zero, Japan's best fighter, was fast and heavily armed

MISSION XTREME 3D

FIGHTER ACES

Q1. Name a famous WWII air battle.

Q2. What do the letters RAF stand for?

Q3. Name two American WWII fighters.

Q4. Which European jet fighter has just come into service?

DEBRIEF

North American P-51D 'Mustang'

P-47 "Thunderbolt"

Messerschmitt BF-109

Supermarine's legendary Spitfire

NOT SO VERY LONG AGO pilots took to the air in frail, unreliable aircraft that often needed brute strength and a lot of luck to control. But things have changed since those early days of aerial warfare. Today's fighter pilots take off in multi-million dollar machines packed with the latest electronics and technology. Some of today's most modern planes can almost fly themselves!

EF 2000 76

Eurofighter "Typhoon" – the world's most advanced fighter

Safely back after a gruelling flight

Debrief answers: 1. The Battle of Britain 2. Royal Air Force 3. P-51D Mustang, P-47 Thunderbolt 4. Eurofighter Typhoon.

military
HEAVYWEIGHTS

> HEAVY TRANSPORT aircraft deliver troops, vehicles and all kind of support equipment to the battlefield. Flying into dangerous conflict situations these aircraft perhaps more than any others need to be strong, fast and reliable. The Lockheed C-130 pictured above and below is the best known example flying today.

This Chinook twin rotor helicopter can drop troops and equipment where landing an airplane would be impossible.

MISSION XTREME 3D

MILITARY HEAVYWEIGHTS

Q1. Why was Boeing's B-17 nicknamed the "Flying Fortress?"

Q2. Which British aircraft was famous for making night-time bombing raids?

Q3. What sort of things do military transport planes carry?

DEBRIEF

A C-130 "Hercules" helps deploy troops to the front line

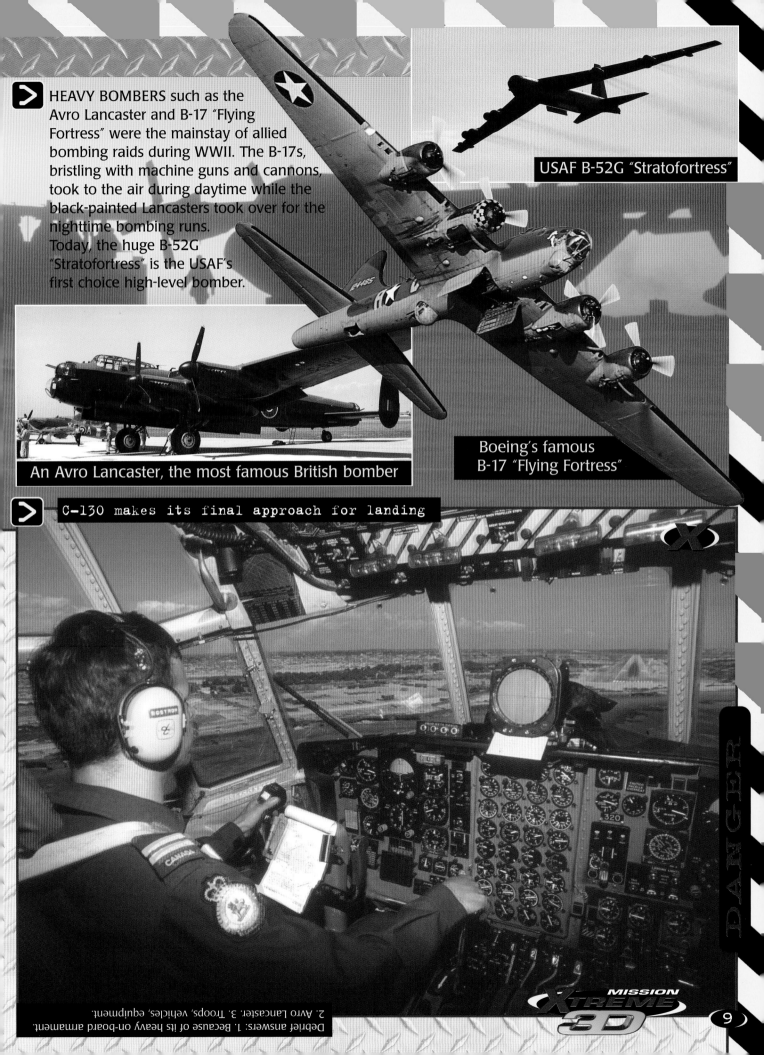

HEAVY BOMBERS such as the Avro Lancaster and B-17 "Flying Fortress" were the mainstay of allied bombing raids during WWII. The B-17s, bristling with machine guns and cannons, took to the air during daytime while the black-painted Lancasters took over for the nighttime bombing runs.
Today, the huge B-52G "Stratofortress" is the USAF's first choice high-level bomber.

USAF B-52G "Stratofortress"

An Avro Lancaster, the most famous British bomber

Boeing's famous B-17 "Flying Fortress"

C-130 makes its final approach for landing

Debrief answers: 1. Because of its heavy on-board armament. 2. Avro Lancaster. 3. Troops, vehicles, equipment.

Is the International Space Station (ISS) the launch pad for future space exploration?

DESTINATION *space*

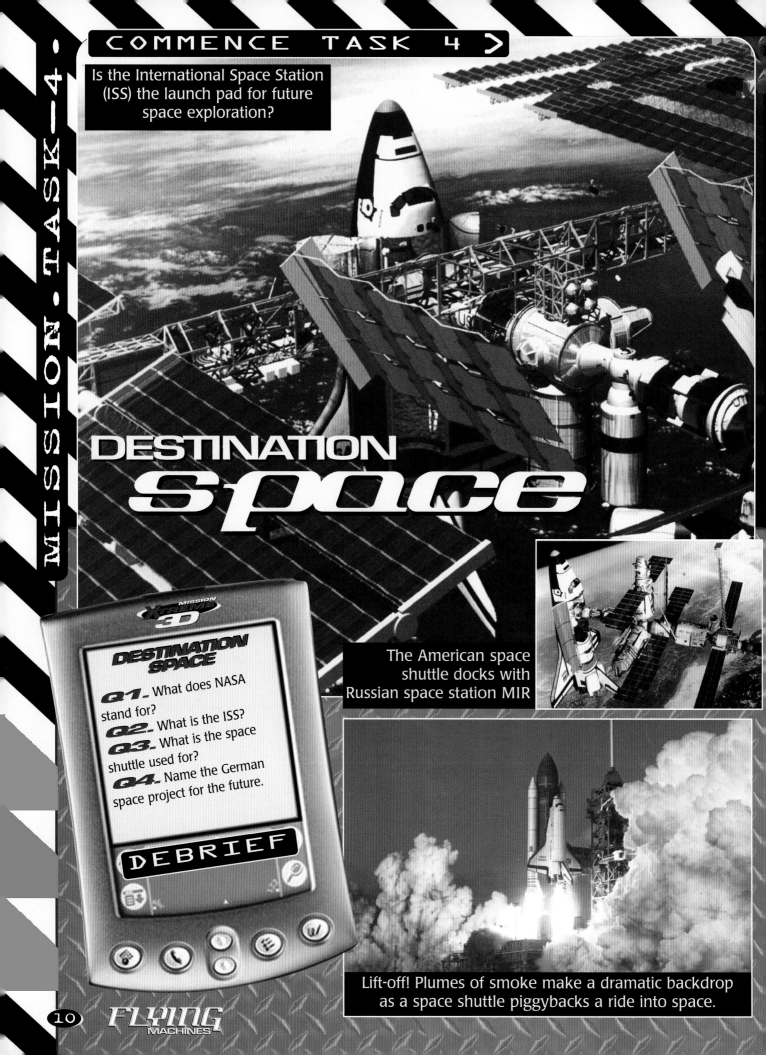

DESTINATION SPACE

Q1. What does NASA stand for?

Q2. What is the ISS?

Q3. What is the space shuttle used for?

Q4. Name the German space project for the future.

DEBRIEF

The American space shuttle docks with Russian space station MIR

Lift-off! Plumes of smoke make a dramatic backdrop as a space shuttle piggybacks a ride into space.

FLYING MACHINES

X-33 experimental space plane

The HL-10 (above) was an early space shuttle prototype

> OVER THE YEARS America's National Aeronautics and Space Administration (NASA) has had its ups and downs. The recent tragedy of the space shuttle Columbia has not dampened its spirit of adventure and determination to take mankind's exploration of space forward. The versatile shuttles are ideal for transporting satellites and equipment into space and are currently helping the construction of the International Space Station – possibly the most important project yet! The future of near Earth space transport lies with reusable winged spacecraft – developing on the shuttle theme. For example, the German Saenger project aims to have a reusable rocket to launch a smaller space plane on missions around the earth and beyond!

The German Saenger rocket launching the smaller Horus space plane

> Gemini 6 and 7 prepare to dock head on.

Debrief answers: 1. National Aeronautics Space Administration. 2. International Space Station. 3. Transport satellites and equipment into space. 4. Saenger.

MISSION XTREME 3D

water BIRDS

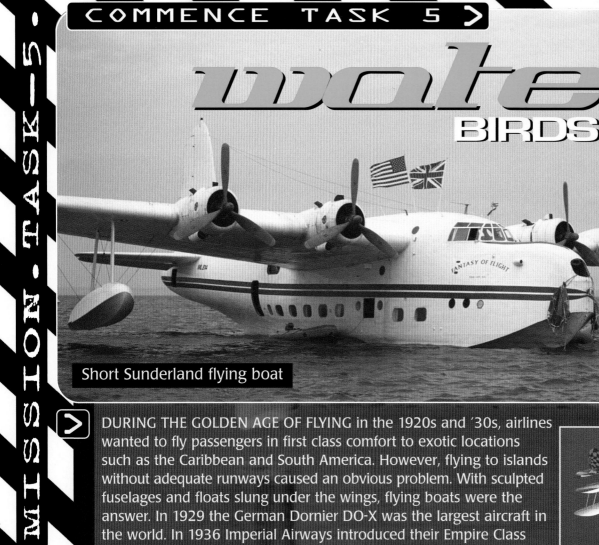

Short Sunderland flying boat

DURING THE GOLDEN AGE OF FLYING in the 1920s and '30s, airlines wanted to fly passengers in first class comfort to exotic locations such as the Caribbean and South America. However, flying to islands without adequate runways caused an obvious problem. With sculpted fuselages and floats slung under the wings, flying boats were the answer. In 1929 the German Dornier DO-X was the largest aircraft in the world. In 1936 Imperial Airways introduced their Empire Class flying boats made by the Irish aircraft manufacturer Short. They immediately became the preferred mode of air transport for upperclass travelers.

1933 Waco UBF-2

An Italian Savoia-Marchetti S-56

MISSION XTREME 3D

WATER BIRDS

Q1. Which company operated the Empire Class flying boats?

Q2. Which flying boat was built in greater numbers than any other?

Q3. Why do planes on aircraft carriers have folding wings?

DEBRIEF

Volmer Sportsman, 1981

The popular Consolidated Catalina

A WWII carrier-based Douglas Skyraider. The wings are folded to save space on the flight deck and also when using the elevator to the service deck.

THE UNIQUE ABILITIES of flying boats make them ideal for the military and emergency services. Used extensively in air-sea rescue and anti-submarine warfare, the Catalina was built in greater numbers than any other flying boat in history. Short Sunderlands joined British Coastal Command hunting German U-Boats. Other planes not equipped to land on the sea can still operate from it. Naval aircraft carriers provide seaborne runways allowing raids to be flown from almost anywhere. These days, the majority of flying boats are in civil use providing, for example, island-hopping taxi services and important links for people living in remote areas around the world.

> This De Havilland Beaver is ideal for wilderness taxi work

N5978

Debrief answers: 1. Imperial Airways, 2. Consolidated Catalina. 3. For storage or using the service elevator.

MISSION XTREME 3D

13

INTERNATIONAL rescue

A tough de Havilland Buffalo sets off on another dangerous rescue mission

Packed full of hi-tech electronics, the Nimrod is probably the world's best maritime patrol aircraft

MISSION XTREME 3D

INTERNATIONAL RESCUE

Q1. What character from Greek mythology is the Lockheed C-130 named after?

Q2. Why is a helicopter a good rescue aircraft?

Q3. Name an aerial firefighter.

Q4. Name a maritime patrol aircraft.

DEBRIEF

> A HELICOPTER'S ability to hover on the spot is extremely useful, especially during an air-sea rescue. The aircraft hovers as specially trained aircrew are lowered to the water, often in extremely dangerous conditions, to rescue stricken sailors.

Aérospatiale HH65A Dolphin search and rescue helicopter

An RAF Sikorsky Sea King returns after another successful rescue at sea

FLYING MACHINES

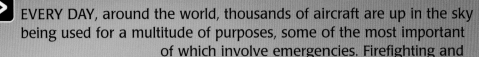

EVERY DAY, around the world, thousands of aircraft are up in the sky being used for a multitude of purposes, some of the most important of which involve emergencies. Firefighting and air-sea rescue are two good examples of situations where aircraft can prove to be real life savers!

C-130s can deliver the goods just about anywhere – even when there isn't a proper runway! The Hercules on the left makes a slow, low-level pass to drop important supplies.

The Canadair CL-415 "Firebird" (below) is a great aircraft. Designed to tackle forest fires in situations far too hazardous for the firefighters on the ground, the Firebirds fly low over rivers and lakes, scooping up thousands of litres of water in a few seconds. They then fly off to attack the fire by dumping the water from huge onboard storage tanks. The CL-415's talents don't end there. It is also extremely useful as an air-sea rescue plane.

Debrief answers: 1. Hercules, 2. It can hover.
3. Canadair CL-415 Firebird 4. Nimrod.

MISSION XTREME 3D

15

DANGER

high PERFORMERS

A Lockheed SR-71 Blackbird high-altitude spyplane waiting for clearance to take off

Spanish Aviojets on a low-level pass

> SPY PLANES such as Lockheed's U2 and SR-71 "Blackbird" operate on the very edge of space. Using ultra-high resolution cameras they photograph military movements on the ground – from over 10 miles (16km) high!

Stopped in its tracks! A McDonnell-Douglas CF-18A Hornet performs a standing stall at Farnborough air show.

The RAF Red Arrows make a dramatic entrance at a public air display

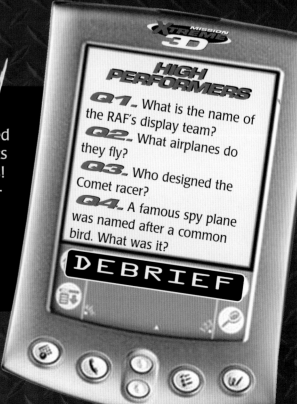

MISSION XTREME 3D

HIGH PERFORMERS

Q1. What is the name of the RAF's display team?

Q2. What airplanes do they fly?

Q3. Who designed the Comet racer?

Q4. A famous spy plane was named after a common bird. What was it?

DEBRIEF

The Red Arrows perform a parasol break in their BAe Hawk trainers

Parachutists enjoy extreme high-altitude thrills

A perfect barrel-roll

HIGH SPEED FLYING ACTION has existed right from the very first take off. By the mid-1900s aircraft like Geoffrey de Havilland's Comet were born from the race for air speed supremacy – their streamlined aerodynamic shapes pointed to the future. When the sound barrier was finally broken in 1947 by Chuck Yeager flying a Bell X-1 rocket plane there seemed to be no limit to what people could achieve. But speed isn't everything. Aerobatic pilots exhibit incredible flying skills using small, highly maneuverable piston engined planes to put on their breathtaking high flying performances.

de Havilland Comet racer

Italian Aermacchi inverted at the top of a loop

MISSION XTREME 3D

MISSION.TASK-8.

Future FLYERS

> DEVELOPMENTS IN CIVIL AVIATION include the Rutan Vari-Eze. Lightweight, efficient and affordable, a reusable rocket version is planned for the near future. At the other end of the scale, NASA is developing a HyperSonic plane that will use revolutionary engines allowing great weight savings and speeds of up to Mach 7. Flying time from London to Tokyo could be as low as just two hours! The Airbus A380 – a double-decker airliner capable of carrying over 500 passengers at over 500mph – could take to the skies as soon as 2006.

Is the Rutan Vari-Eze the shape of things to come?

MISSION XTREME 3D

FUTURE FLYERS

Q1. A double-decker airliner is due for introduction in 2006. What is it called?

Q2. Who is developing a hypersonic plane?

Q3. How fast will it fly?

Q4. How much do B-2 Stealth bombers cost?

DEBRIEF

Satic A300-600ST Beluga super transport

An Airbus A380 "double decker" airliner

FLYING MACHINES

B2 stealth bomber: the world's most expensive aircraft

McDonnell-Douglas 21st century fighter

Eurofighter Typhoon

> IN THE WORLD of military aviation, developments in speed and maneuvreability do not come cheap. The USAF use some of the world's most expensive aircraft. At 100 million dollars each, American F22 Interceptors seem cheap compared with the B-2 Stealth bomber, the most expensive plane in service at 2 billion dollars apiece!

F-117 "Nighthawk" Stealth fighter

The latest Merlin helicopter can virtually fly itself

Apache AH64 attack helicopter

Debrief answers: 1. Airbus A380. 2. NASA. 3. Mach 7. 4. Two billion dollars each.

MISSION XTREME 3D

19